# Celiac Dise

# COOKBOOK FOR KIDS

*A Beginners Guide For Newly Diagnosed Young Warriors,*
*Featuring Nutrition Diet Recipes, Fun Meal Prep*

**Amelia Sophia**

# TABLE OF CONTENT

# GET YOUR 7 DAYS MEAL PLAN AND 4 WEEKS MEAL PLNNER JOURNAL AT THE END OF THE BOOK

**AMELIA SOPHIA
1 WEEK MEAL PLAN**

**AMELIA SOPHIA
WEEKLY FOOD JOURNAL**

# PLEASE DONT FORGET TO LEAVE YOUR HONEST REVIEW

## INTRODUCTION

Hello there, fellow kitchen explorers! Welcome to "Gluten-Free Adventures," a culinary journey designed especially for the bravest little chefs and their superhero parents. If you're flipping through these pages, chances are you're part of the incredible team supporting a kid with celiac disease.

Living with celiac disease can be a challenge, but it doesn't mean the end of delicious meals and fantastic food experiences. In fact, it's the beginning of a new and exciting adventure in the kitchen. This cookbook is your trusty guide, filled with tasty recipes that will make every meal a celebration of flavors, textures, and, most importantly, good health.

As we embark on this gluten-free culinary journey together, we'll discover creative and scrumptious ways to navigate the world of gluten-free cooking. Whether your little one is a budding chef or simply loves to munch on tasty treats, these recipes are crafted with love, simplicity, and a dash of fun.

So, grab your aprons, roll up your sleeves, and get ready for a cooking expedition that will not only fill tummies but also warm hearts. Let's turn every meal into a gluten-free adventure that the whole family can enjoy. Happy cooking!

# IMPORTANT NOTICE

## A Friendly Heads-Up about Ingredient Portions in Our Recipes!

We wanted to drop you a quick note about a little something that might make a big difference in your cooking experience.

You know how we're all about delicious, healthy meals, right? Well, it turns out that some of the ingredients we use are best enjoyed in moderation. Think of them like the occasional treat - totally fine in small doses, but maybe not the best idea to go all-in.

*Research has shown that certain foods, when consumed in excess, might not be the best pals for our health. We're talking about those sneaky ingredients that can be a bit naughty if we overindulge. But fear not, it's all about balance!*

So, here's the scoop: when you see those ingredients marked with a little caution sign or a friendly reminder in our recipes, it's like a little nudge from us saying, "Hey, enjoy, but maybe not too much of this good thing!"

Remember, life's all about balance and enjoying the journey, especially when it comes to food. Feel free to tweak the portions to suit your taste buds and dietary goals. After all, cooking is an art, not a strict science.

Thanks a bunch for being part of our food-loving community. We're here to make your culinary experience not only delicious but also a breeze.

# CHAPTER 1

# UNDERSTANDING CELIAC DISEASE FOR KIDS:

Celiac disease is not merely a dietary preference but a medical condition that affects the digestive system. In simple terms for our young readers, it means that certain foods can make the tummy feel unwell. More precisely, when kids with celiac disease eat gluten, a protein found in wheat, barley, and rye, it triggers an immune response that damages the small intestine.

Now, why is the small intestine so crucial? It's like the body's nutrient highway. When damaged, it hinders the body's ability to absorb essential nutrients, leading to a variety of health issues, such as stunted growth, fatigue, and stomach pain.

## A Historical Perspective on the Gluten-Free Diet

The gluten-free diet's history is fascinating, rooted in the early 20th century when the connection between wheat consumption and celiac disease was first recognized. However, it wasn't until the 1940s that Dr. Willem-Karel Dicke, a Dutch pediatrician, made a groundbreaking discovery during World War II. In times of food scarcity, he observed that children with celiac disease improved when wheat was scarce, leading to the identification of gluten as the culprit.

Over subsequent decades, scientific understanding and diagnostic methods advanced, cementing the role of gluten in celiac disease. The 21st century witnessed a surge in gluten-free awareness, with a plethora of gluten-free products flooding the market. Today, the gluten-free diet is not just a medical necessity but a lifestyle choice for many, spurred by increased awareness of gluten sensitivity and the perceived health benefits of reducing gluten intake.

## Benefits of a Gluten-Free Diet for Kids:

**Improved Digestive Health:**

A gluten-free diet is the cornerstone of managing celiac disease. By eliminating gluten, the small intestine can gradually heal, improving digestion and ensuring that nutrients are absorbed properly. This sets the stage for better overall health and growth in children.

**Enhanced Energy Levels:**

Kids need energy for their vibrant activities and growth. A gluten-free diet can help alleviate fatigue and boost energy levels by promoting optimal nutrient absorption. When the body receives the right fuel, it performs at its best, enabling children to thrive in their daily adventures.

**Promotion of Healthy Growth:**

Children with celiac disease may experience growth issues due to malabsorption of nutrients. A gluten-free diet can aid in restoring healthy growth patterns by addressing the underlying cause. Proper nutrition supports the development of strong bones, muscles, and overall physical well-being.

## Mood and Cognitive Benefits:

Research indicates a potential link between gluten sensitivity and mood disorders in some individuals. By adhering to a gluten-free diet, children may experience improved mood and cognitive function. A well-nourished brain contributes to better focus, memory, and overall mental well-being.

## Prevention of Long-Term Complications:

Unmanaged celiac disease can lead to serious long-term complications, including an increased risk of autoimmune disorders and certain cancers. A gluten-free diet acts as a preventive measure, reducing the like hood of these complications and fostering a healthier future for your child.

# CHAPTR 2

# BREAKFAST RECIPES

*Gluten-Free Pancakes with Almond Flour*

**Serves: 4**

**Cooking Time: 15 minutes**

**Ingredients:**

- 1 cup almond flour
- 2 tablespoons maple syrup
- 1 teaspoon baking powder
- 1/2 teaspoon vanilla extract
- 2 large eggs
- 1/2 cup milk (dairy-free if needed)
- Butter or oil for cooking

**Instructions:**

- In a bowl, mix almond flour, maple syrup, baking powder, vanilla extract, eggs, and milk until you have a smooth batter.

- Heat a pan over medium heat and add a small amount of butter or oil.
- Pour small amounts of batter onto the pan to form pancakes.
- Cook until bubbles form on the surface, then flip and cook the other side until golden brown.
- Serve with your favorite toppings like fresh berries or a dollop of yogurt.

**Note (Ingredient Avoidance):**

*Kids should avoid regular wheat flour because it can upset the tummy for those with Celiac Disease. Instead, we use almond flour, which is gentle and gluten-free!*

**Serving Suggestion:**

*Top your pancakes with colorful berries or make funny face shapes with fruit slices for a delightful breakfast!*

**Nutritional Information:**

- Calories: 180 per serving
- Protein: 7g per serving
- Carbohydrates: 12g per serving

- Fat: 13g per serving
- Fiber: 3g per serving

## *Quinoa Breakfast Bowl with Fruits and Nuts*

**Serves: 2**

**Cooking Time: 20 minutes**

**Ingredients:**

- 1 cup quinoa
- 2 cups water
- 1 cup mixed fruits (berries, banana slices)
- 1/4 cup chopped nuts (almonds, walnuts)
- 2 tablespoons honey

**Instructions:**

- Rinse quinoa under cold water and cook it with 2 cups of water until fluffy.
- Let it cool, then mix in fruits and nuts.
- Drizzle honey on top and stir gently.

**Note (Ingredient Avoidance):**

*Kids should avoid wheat-based cereals. Instead, we use quinoa, which is like tiny magic seeds that are safe and delicious!*

**Serving Suggestion:**

*Add a sprinkle of colorful sprinkles for a fun and tasty morning treat!*

**Nutritional Information:**

- Calories: 300 per serving
- Protein: 9g per serving
- Carbohydrates: 50g per serving
- Fat: 7g per serving
- Fiber: 6g per serving

# Rice Flour Crepes with Strawberry Filling

**Serves: 6**

**Cooking Time: 25 minutes**

**Ingredients:**

- 1 cup rice flour
- 2 cups milk (dairy-free if needed)
- 2 large eggs
- 1/4 cup melted butter
- 1 cup sliced strawberries
- Powdered sugar for dusting

**Instructions:**

- Mix rice flour, milk, eggs, and melted butter to make a smooth batter.
- Heat a non-stick pan and pour a thin layer of batter.
- Cook until the edges lift, flip, and cook the other side.
- Fill with sliced strawberries, roll, and dust with powdered sugar.

**Note (Ingredient Avoidance):**

*Kids should avoid wheat-based pancakes. Instead, we use rice flour, which makes our crepes light and safe for little tummies!*

**Serving Suggestion:**

*Serve with a dollop of whipped cream or a side of yogurt for extra yum!*

**Nutritional Information:**

- Calories: 150 per serving
- Protein: 5g per serving
- Carbohydrates: 20g per serving
- Fat: 6g per serving
- Fiber: 1g per serving

# Buckwheat Waffles Topped with Blueberries

**Serves: 4**

**Cooking Time: 20 minutes**

**Ingredients:**

- 1 cup buckwheat flour
- 1 tablespoon sugar
- 1 teaspoon baking powder
- 1/2 teaspoon cinnamon
- 1 cup milk (dairy-free if needed)
- 2 tablespoons melted butter
- Blueberries for topping

**Instructions:**

- Mix buckwheat flour, sugar, baking powder, cinnamon, milk, and melted butter until smooth.
- Pour the batter into a preheated waffle maker and cook until golden.
- Top with a handful of fresh blueberries.

**Note (Ingredient Avoidance):**

*Kids should avoid regular waffles with wheat. Instead, we use magical buckwheat to make our waffles extra tasty and safe!*

**Serving Suggestion:**

*Drizzle a bit of honey or maple syrup for a sweet touch, and don't forget to share with friends!*

**Nutritional Information:**

- Calories: 220 per serving
- Protein: 6g per serving
- Carbohydrates: 30g per serving
- Fat: 9g per serving
- Fiber: 3g per serving

# Millet Porridge with Cinnamon and Apples

**Serves: 4**

**Cooking Time: 15 minutes**

**Ingredients:**

- 1 cup millet
- 3 cups water
- 1/2 cup milk (dairy-free if needed)
- 1/4 cup honey
- 1 teaspoon cinnamon
- 1 cup diced apples

**Instructions:**

- Rinse millet under cold water and cook it with water until tender.
- Stir in milk, honey, cinnamon, and diced apples.
- Simmer until it thickens and apples soften.

**Note (Ingredient Avoidance):**

*Kids should avoid oatmeal with gluten. Instead, we use millet to make our porridge warm, cozy, and gluten-free!*

**Serving Suggestion:**

*Sprinkle a little extra cinnamon on top or add a few raisins for a tasty twist!*

**Nutritional Information:**

- Calories: 180 per serving
- Protein: 4g per serving
- Carbohydrates: 40g per serving
- Fat: 2g per serving
- Fiber: 5g per serving

# Sorghum Cereal with Banana Slices

**Serves: 2**

**Cooking Time: 15 minutes**

**Ingredients:**

- 1 cup sorghum cereal
- 1 banana, sliced
- 2 cups milk (check for gluten-free label)

**Instructions:**

- Pour sorghum cereal into a bowl.
- Add milk and top with banana slices.
- Stir gently and enjoy!

**Note (Ingredient Avoidance):**

*KIDS SHOULD AVOID regular wheat cereal if they have Celiac Disease. Instead, choose cereals made from sorghum or other gluten-free grains.*

**Serving Suggestion:**

*Serve with a side of yogurt or a sprinkle of gluten-free granola for added crunch.*

## Nutritional Information:

- Calories: 250 per serving
- Protein: 5g per serving
- Carbohydrates: 50g per serving
- Fat: 3g per serving
- Fiber: 6g per serving

## *Teff Muffins with Raspberries*

**Serves: 6**

**Cooking Time: 20 minutes**

**Ingredients:**

- 1 cup teff flour
- 1/2 cup sugar
- 1/2 cup butter, melted
- 1/2 cup milk (check for gluten-free label)
- 1 tsp baking powder
- 1/2 cup fresh raspberries

**Instructions:**

- Preheat oven to 375° F (190° C).

- In a bowl, mix teff flour, sugar, melted butter, milk, and baking powder.
- Gently fold in raspberries.
- Spoon batter into muffin cups and bake for 15-20 minutes.

## Note (Ingredient Avoidance):

*KIDS SHOULD AVOID regular wheat flour if they have Celiac Disease. Instead, use teff flour or other gluten-free flour alternatives.*

## Serving Suggestion:

*Serve with a dollop of whipped cream or a side of fresh fruit.*

## Nutritional Information:

- Calories: 200 per muffin
- Protein: 3g per muffin
- Carbohydrates: 25g per muffin
- Fat: 10g per muffin
- Fiber: 4g per muffin

# Coconut Flour Smoothie Bowl with Mango and Kiwi

**Serves: 1**

**Prep Time: 10 minutes**

**Ingredients:**

- 2 tbsp coconut flour
- 1 cup coconut milk (check for gluten-free label)
- 1/2 mango, diced
- 1 kiwi, sliced

**Instructions:**

- In a bowl, mix coconut flour with coconut milk until smooth.
- Top with diced mango and sliced kiwi.

**Note (Ingredient Avoidance):**

*KIDS SHOULD AVOID regular wheat flour if they have Celiac Disease. Coconut flour is a tasty gluten-free alternative.*

**Serving Suggestion:**

*Sprinkle with shredded coconut or gluten-free granola for extra flavor.*

**Nutritional Information:**

- Calories: 300 per serving
- Protein: 5g per serving
- Carbohydrates: 40g per serving
- Fat: 15g per serving
- Fiber: 8g per serving

# Polenta Breakfast Casserole with Spinach and Feta

**Serves: 4**

**Cooking Time: 30 minutes**

**Ingredients:**

- 1 cup polenta
- 2 cups water
- 1 cup spinach, chopped
- 1/2 cup feta cheese, crumbled
- Salt and pepper to taste

**Instructions:**

- Cook polenta in water according to package instructions.
- Mix in chopped spinach and crumbled feta.
- Bake in a casserole dish for 20 minutes.

**Note (Ingredient Avoidance):**

*KIDS SHOULD AVOID regular wheat-based grains if they have Celiac Disease. Opt for polenta made from corn for a gluten-free choice.*

**Serving Suggestion:**

*Top with a fried egg or fresh herbs for a delightful twist.*

**Nutritional Information:**

- Calories: 180 per serving
- Protein: 5g per serving
- Carbohydrates: 30g per serving
- Fat: 6g per serving
- Fiber: 3g per serving

## Almond Meal Banana Bread

**Serves: 8**

**Cooking Time: 45 minutes**

**Ingredients:**

- 2 cups almond meal
- 3 ripe bananas, mashed
- 1/4 cup honey
- 3 eggs
- 1 tsp baking soda
- 1/2 tsp vanilla extract

**Instructions:**

- Preheat oven to 350° F (175° C).
- Mix almond meal, mashed bananas, honey, eggs, baking soda, and vanilla extract.
- Pour into a greased loaf pan and bake for 40-45 minutes.

## Note (Ingredient Avoidance):

*KIDS SHOULD AVOID regular wheat flour if they have Celiac Disease. Almond meal is a wonderful gluten-free substitute.*

## Serving Suggestion:

*Spread with almond butter or enjoy with a glass of milk.*

## Nutritional Information:

- Calories: 220 per serving
- Protein: 7g per serving
- Carbohydrates: 20g per serving
- Fat: 14g per serving
- Fiber: 4g per serving

# CHAPTER 3

# LUNCH RECIPES

*Quinoa-Stuffed Bell Peppers with Ground Turkey and Veggies*

**Serves: 4**

**Cooking Time: 45 minutes**

**Ingredients:**

- 4 bell peppers (any color), halved and seeded
- 1 cup quinoa, rinsed
- 1 pound ground turkey
- 1 onion, diced
- 2 cloves garlic, minced
- 1 cup mixed veggies (carrots, peas, corn)
- 1 cup tomato sauce
- Salt and pepper to taste
- Olive oil

## Instructions:

- Preheat the oven to 375° F (190° C).
- Boil quinoa according to package instructions. Set aside.
- In a pan, cook ground turkey until browned. Set aside.
- In the same pan, sauté onions and garlic until soft. Add mixed veggies and cook until tender.
- Combine cooked quinoa, turkey, veggies, tomato sauce, salt, and pepper in a bowl.
- Rub bell pepper halves with olive oil and stuff them with the quinoa mixture.
- Place stuffed peppers in a baking dish, cover with foil, and bake for 25-30 minutes.

## Note (Ingredient Avoidance):

*Kids should avoid wheat, barley, and rye because they have gluten that can make tummies unhappy. Instead of breadcrumbs, we're using quinoa, which is safe and super yummy!*

**Serving Suggestion:**

*Serve these colorful stuffed peppers with a side of fresh salad or steamed veggies*

**Nutritional Information:**

- Calories: 350 per serving
- Protein: 25g per serving
- Carbohydrates: 30g per serving
- Fat: 12g per serving
- Fiber: 6g per serving

## Rice Noodle Stir-Fry with Gluten-Free Soy Sauce and Vegetables

**Serves: 4**

**Cooking Time: 30 minutes**

**Ingredients:**

- 8 oz rice noodles
- 1 cup broccoli florets
- 1 carrot, julienned
- 1 bell pepper, thinly sliced

- 1 cup snap peas
- 1 lb chicken breast, thinly sliced (optional)
- 3 tablespoons gluten-free soy sauce
- 2 tablespoons sesame oil
- 2 cloves garlic, minced
- 1 tablespoon ginger, grated
- Sesame seeds for garnish

**Instructions:**

- Cook rice noodles according to package instructions. Drain and set aside.
- In a large pan, heat sesame oil over medium heat. Add garlic and ginger, sauté until fragrant.
- Add chicken (if using) and cook until browned. Add vegetables and stir-fry until tender-crisp.
- Toss in cooked rice noodles and pour gluten-free soy sauce over the mixture. Stir to combine.
- Cook for an additional 3-5 minutes until everything is heated through.
- Garnish with sesame seeds and serve.

**Note (Ingredient Avoidance):**

*Kids should avoid regular soy sauce because it contains gluten. We're using a special gluten-free soy sauce so everyone can enjoy this delicious stir-fry safely!*

**Serving Suggestion:**

*Serve this colorful stir-fry on a plate or in a fun bowl. Add chopsticks for extra fun!*

**Nutritional Information:**

- Calories: 380 per serving
- Protein: 20g per serving
- Carbohydrates: 50g per serving
- Fat: 12g per serving
- Fiber: 5g per serving

# Lentil and Vegetable Curry with Basmati Rice

**Serves: 4**

**Cooking Time: 40 minutes**

**Ingredients:**

- 1 cup dry lentils, rinsed
- 1 onion, finely chopped
- 2 carrots, diced
- 1 zucchini, diced
- 1 cup cauliflower florets
- 1 cup coconut milk
- 2 tablespoons curry powder
- 1 teaspoon turmeric
- 1 teaspoon cumin
- 1 cup basmati rice, cooked
- Fresh cilantro for garnish
- Salt and pepper to taste

**Instructions:**

- Cook lentils in a pot with water until tender. Drain and set aside.

- In a large pan, sauté onions until golden. Add carrots, zucchini, and cauliflower.
- Stir in curry powder, turmeric, and cumin. Cook until veggies are tender.
- Add cooked lentils and coconut milk. Simmer for 10 minutes.
- Season with salt and pepper to taste.
- Serve over a bed of basmati rice and garnish with fresh cilantro.

## Note (Ingredient Avoidance):

*Kids should avoid lentils if they're not feeling well. You can replace lentils with chickpeas; they're just as tasty and gentle on tummies!*

## Serving Suggestion:

*Serve this curry in a colorful bowl with a side of fluffy basmati rice. Don't forget to make a smiley face with the rice!*

## Nutritional Information:

- Calories: 320 per serving
- Protein: 15g per serving

- Carbohydrates: 45g per serving
- Fat: 8g per serving
- Fiber: 10g per serving

## Zucchini Noodles with Gluten-Free Tomato Sauce and Grilled Chicken

**Serves: 4**

**Cooking Time: 25 minutes**

**Ingredients:**

- 4 medium-sized zucchini
- 1 lb chicken breast, grilled and sliced
- 2 cups gluten-free tomato sauce
- 1 tablespoon olive oil
- 2 cloves garlic, minced
- 1 teaspoon dried oregano
- 1 teaspoon dried basil
- Salt and pepper to taste
- Grated Parmesan cheese for garnish (optional)

## Instructions:

- Using a spiralizer, make zucchini noodles from the zucchinis. Set aside.
- In a pan, heat olive oil over medium heat. Add minced garlic and sauté until fragrant.
- Add zucchini noodles and toss until they are just tender but still have a nice crunch.
- Pour in gluten-free tomato sauce, dried oregano, and dried basil. Stir until heated through.
- Season with salt and pepper to taste.
- Serve the zucchini noodles topped with grilled chicken slices. Sprinkle with Parmesan cheese if desired.

## Note (Ingredient Avoidance):

*Kids should avoid regular pasta because it has gluten. Zucchini noodles are a cool and tasty substitute that won't upset tummies!*

## Serving Suggestion:

*Serve this dish in a fun plate with the zucchini noodles forming a smiley face. It makes eating veggies more exciting!*

**Nutritional Information:**

- Calories: 280 per serving
- Protein: 25g per serving
- Carbohydrates: 15g per serving
- Fat: 10g per serving
- Fiber: 5g per serving

## *Buckwheat and Vegetable Sushi Rolls*

**Serves: 4**

**Cooking Time: 45 minutes**

**Ingredients:**

- 1 cup buckwheat groats, cooked
- 4 sheets nori (seaweed)
- 1 cucumber, julienned
- 1 carrot, julienned
- 1 avocado, sliced
- 1/2 pound cooked shrimp or imitation crab (optional)
- Gluten-free soy sauce for dipping
- Pickled ginger and wasabi for serving

## Instructions:

- Cook buckwheat groats according to package instructions. Let them cool.
- Place a sheet of nori on a bamboo sushi rolling mat.
- Spread a thin layer of cooked buckwheat over the nori.
- Arrange cucumber, carrot, avocado, and shrimp or imitation crab along the edge of the nori.
- Roll the nori tightly using the bamboo mat. Seal the edge with a little water.
- Slice the roll into bite-sized pieces with a sharp knife.
- Repeat with the remaining ingredients.
- Serve with gluten-free soy sauce, pickled ginger, and wasabi.

## Note (Ingredient Avoidance):

*Kids should avoid regular sushi rice as it contains gluten. We're using buckwheat instead, which is just as yummy and safe for your tummy!*

**Serving Suggestion:**

*Serve these sushi rolls on a colorful plate with small bowls of soy sauce, pickled ginger, and wasabi. It's like a tasty rainbow on your plate!*

**Nutritional Information:**

- Calories: 220 per serving
- Protein: 10g per serving
- Carbohydrates: 40g per serving
- Fat: 5g per serving
- Fiber: 8g per serving

# Millet and Black Bean Salad with Lime Vinaigrette

**Serves: 4**

**Cooking Time: 30 minutes**

**Ingredients:**

- 1 cup millet, cooked
- 1 can black beans, drained and rinsed
- 1 cup cherry tomatoes, halved
- 1/2 cup cucumber, diced
- 1/4 cup red onion, finely chopped
- 2 tablespoons fresh cilantro, chopped
- 2 tablespoons lime juice
- 3 tablespoons olive oil
- Salt and pepper to taste

**Instructions:**

- In a large bowl, mix together cooked millet, black beans, cherry tomatoes, cucumber, red onion, and cilantro.

- In a small bowl, whisk together lime juice, olive oil, salt, and pepper to make the vinaigrette.
- Pour the vinaigrette over the salad and toss until well combined.
- Chill in the refrigerator for at least 15 minutes before serving.

## Note (Ingredient Avoidance):

*Kids should avoid wheat, barley, and rye because they have gluten that can make tummies unhappy. Millet is a super tasty and safe grain for our salad!*

## Serving Suggestion:

*Serve this refreshing salad as a side dish or enjoy it on its own.*

## Nutritional Information:

- Calories: 220 per serving
- Protein: 7g per serving
- Carbohydrates: 35g per serving
- Fat: 6g per serving
- Fiber: 8g per serving

# Sorghum Grain Bowl with Roasted Vegetables and Tahini Dressing

**Serves: 4**

**Cooking Time: 40 minutes**

**Ingredients:**

- 1 cup sorghum, cooked
- 2 cups mixed vegetables (carrots, broccoli, bell peppers), chopped
- 2 tablespoons olive oil
- Salt and pepper to taste
- 1/4 cup tahini
- 2 tablespoons lemon juice
- 1 clove garlic, minced
- Fresh parsley for garnish

**Instructions:**

- Preheat the oven to 400° F (200° C).
- Toss mixed vegetables with olive oil, salt, and pepper. Roast in the oven for 20-25 minutes until golden.

- In a bowl, mix cooked sorghum and roasted vegetables.
- In a small bowl, whisk together tahini, lemon juice, and minced garlic to make the dressing.
- Drizzle the tahini dressing over the grain bowl and toss until everything is coated.
- Garnish with fresh parsley before serving.

## Note (Ingredient Avoidance):

*Kids should avoid wheat, barley, and rye because they have gluten that can make tummies unhappy. Sorghum is a special grain that is safe and yummy for our bowl!*

## Serving Suggestion:

*Enjoy this hearty bowl as a wholesome lunch or dinner.*

## Nutritional Information:

- Calories: 280 per serving
- Protein: 6g per serving
- Carbohydrates: 40g per serving
- Fat: 11g per serving
- Fiber: 6g per serving

# Teff Wraps with Turkey, Avocado, and Lettuce

**Serves: 4**

**Cooking Time: 25 minutes**

**Ingredients:**

- 1 cup teff flour
- 1 1/2 cups water
- 1/2 teaspoon salt
- 1 pound ground turkey, cooked
- 1 avocado, sliced
- 1 cup lettuce, shredded
- Salsa or your favorite gluten-free sauce for topping

**Instructions:**

- In a bowl, mix teff flour, water, and salt to create the batter for the wraps.
- Heat a non-stick pan over medium heat. Pour a small amount of batter to make thin wraps. Cook for 2-3 minutes on each side.
- Once cooked, set aside the teff wraps.

- Fill each wrap with cooked ground turkey, avocado slices, and shredded lettuce.
- Add a dollop of salsa or your favorite gluten-free sauce on top.

**Note (Ingredient Avoidance):**

*Kids should avoid wheat, barley, and rye because they have gluten that can make tummies unhappy. Teff is a magic grain that helps us make delicious wraps without any gluten*!

**Serving Suggestion:**

*These wraps are perfect for lunch or a snack. Roll them up and enjoy!*

**Nutritional Information:**

- Calories: 320 per serving
- Protein: 18g per serving
- Carbohydrates: 30g per serving
- Fat: 15g per serving
- Fiber: 6g per serving

# Coconut Flour-Crusted Chicken Tenders with Sweet Potato Fries

**Serves: 4**

**Cooking Time: 35 minutes**

**Ingredients:**

- 1 pound chicken tenders
- 1/2 cup coconut flour
- 2 eggs, beaten
- 1 cup gluten-free breadcrumbs
- 1 teaspoon garlic powder
- 1 teaspoon paprika
- Salt and pepper to taste
- 2 large sweet potatoes, cut into fries
- 2 tablespoons olive oil
- Ketchup or your favorite gluten-free dipping sauce

**Instructions:**

- Preheat the oven to 400° F (200° C).
- In one bowl, place coconut flour. In another bowl, mix breadcrumbs, garlic powder, paprika, salt, and pepper.

- Dip each chicken tender first into the coconut flour, then into the beaten eggs, and finally into the breadcrumb mixture. Place on a baking sheet.
- Toss sweet potato fries with olive oil, salt, and pepper. Spread them on the same baking sheet.
- Bake in the oven for 20-25 minutes, or until the chicken is cooked through and the sweet potato fries are crispy.

## Note (Ingredient Avoidance):

*Kids should avoid wheat, barley, and rye because they have gluten that can make tummies unhappy. Instead of regular flour, we're using coconut flour, which makes our chicken tenders super tasty!*

## Serving Suggestion:

*Dip these crunchy chicken tenders and sweet potato fries in ketchup or your favorite gluten-free sauce.*

## Nutritional Information:

- Calories: 380 per serving
- Protein: 25g per serving

- Carbohydrates: 35g per serving
- Fat: 15g per serving
- Fiber: 6g per serving

## Polenta Pizza with Tomato, Mozzarella, and Basil

**Serves: 4**

**Cooking Time: 30 minutes**

**Ingredients:**

- 1 cup polenta, cooked and cooled
- 1 cup gluten-free pizza sauce
- 1 1/2 cups mozzarella cheese, shredded
- Cherry tomatoes, sliced
- Fresh basil leaves
- Olive oil
- Salt and pepper to taste

**Instructions:**

- Preheat the oven to 400° F (200° C).
- Spread the cooked polenta on a baking sheet to create a pizza crust.

- Bake for 15-20 minutes or until the edges are golden.
- Remove the polenta crust from the oven and spread gluten-free pizza sauce evenly.
- Sprinkle mozzarella cheese over the sauce and add sliced cherry tomatoes.
- Bake for an additional 10 minutes or until the cheese is melted and bubbly.
- Remove from the oven, sprinkle fresh basil leaves, drizzle with olive oil, and add salt and pepper to taste.

## Note (Ingredient Avoidance):

*Kids should avoid wheat, barley, and rye because they have gluten that can make tummies unhappy. Polenta is our gluten-free hero, making our pizza super yummy without any gluten!*

## Serving Suggestion:

*Cut the polenta pizza into slices and enjoy a gluten-free pizza party!*

## Nutritional Information:

- Calories: 250 per serving
- Protein: 10g per serving

- Carbohydrates: 30g per serving
- Fat: 10g per serving
- Fiber: 4g per serving

## LOVELY READER!

I hope you've been enjoying the adventure within the pages of my book.

Your thoughts mean the world to me, and I'd be absolutely thrilled if you could take a moment to share your honest review. Whether its praise, constructive criticism, or you' re your overall vibes, your words can make a real impact

I noticed those we give free copies or buy this book don' t give their honest reviews and it's disappointing to me

Please can you give me your honest review?

## THANK YOU

# CHAPTER 4

# SNACKS AND APPETIZER

*Rice Cake with Almond Butter and Sliced Strawberries*

**Serves: 2**

**Cooking Time: 5 minutes**

**Ingredients:**

- 4 rice cakes
- 4 tablespoons almond butter
- 1 cup sliced strawberries

**Instructions:**

- Spread almond butter on each rice cake.
- Top with sliced strawberries.

**Note (Ingredient Avoidance):**

*Kids should avoid wheat, barley, and rye because they have gluten that can make tummies unhappy. Instead of regular bread, we use rice cakes, which are like crunchy clouds and totally gluten-free!*

## Serving Suggestion:

*Enjoy these tasty treats as a quick snack or a fun dessert.*

## Nutritional Information:

- Calories: 250 per serving
- Protein: 7g per serving
- Carbohydrates: 30g per serving
- Fat: 12g per serving
- Fiber: 4g per serving

# Quinoa and Black Bean Salsa with Gluten-Free Tortilla Chips

**Serves: 4**

**Cooking Time: 15 minutes**

**Ingredients:**

- 1 cup cooked quinoa
- 1 can black beans, drained and rinsed
- 1 cup corn kernels
- 1 cup diced tomatoes
- 1/2 cup chopped cilantro
- Juice of 1 lime
- Salt and pepper to taste
- Gluten-free tortilla chips

**Instructions:**

- In a large bowl, mix quinoa, black beans, corn, tomatoes, cilantro, lime juice, salt, and pepper.
- Serve with gluten-free tortilla chips for dipping.

**Note (Ingredient Avoidance):**

*Kids should avoid regular tortilla chips because they can have sneaky gluten. Instead, we use gluten-free tortilla chips, which are just as crunchy and way more fun!*

**Serving Suggestion:**

*Turn snack time into a fiesta with this colorful quinoa and black bean salsa.*

**Nutritional Information:**

- Calories: 180 per serving
- Protein: 5g per serving
- Carbohydrates: 35g per serving
- Fat: 2g per serving
- Fiber: 6g per serving

# Buckwheat Crackers with Hummus and Cherry Tomatoes

**Serves: 3**

**Cooking Time: 20 minutes**

**Ingredients:**

- 1 cup buckwheat flour
- 1/4 cup olive oil
- 1/4 cup water
- 1/2 teaspoon salt
- Hummus for dipping
- Cherry tomatoes for topping

**Instructions:**

- Preheat the oven to 350° F (175° C).
- In a bowl, mix buckwheat flour, olive oil, water, and salt to form a dough.
- Roll out the dough and cut into cracker shapes.
- Bake for 15-18 minutes or until golden and crispy.
- Let them cool and serve with hummus and cherry tomatoes.

**Note (Ingredient Avoidance):**

*Kids should avoid regular crackers because they might have gluten hiding in them. Instead, we use buckwheat flour to make our own crackers - they're crunchy and gluten-free!*

**Serving Suggestion:**

*Make snack time exciting with these homemade buckwheat crackers served with hummus and cherry tomatoes.*

**Nutritional Information:**

- Calories: 120 per serving
- Protein: 2g per serving
- Carbohydrates: 15g per serving
- Fat: 6g per serving
- Fiber: 2g per serving

# Millet Energy Bites with Dried Fruit and Seeds

**Serves: 6**

**Cooking Time: 10 minutes**

**Ingredients:**

- 1 cup cooked millet
- 1/2 cup almond butter
- 1/4 cup honey
- 1/4 cup dried fruit (e.g., raisins, cranberries)
- 2 tablespoons chia seeds
- 1/4 cup shredded coconut (optional)

**Instructions:**

- In a bowl, mix millet, almond butter, honey, dried fruit, chia seeds, and shredded coconut.
- Form small balls and refrigerate for 1 hour before serving.

**Note (Ingredient Avoidance):**

*Kids should avoid regular energy bars because they can have gluten. Instead, we make our own with millet, which is a super grain that's totally gluten-free!*

**Serving Suggestion:**

*Pop these energy bites into lunchboxes for a tasty and nutritious treat.*

**Nutritional Information:**

- Calories: 150 per serving
- Protein: 4g per serving
- Carbohydrates: 20g per serving
- Fat: 7g per serving
- Fiber: 2g per serving

# Sorghum Popcorn Balls with a Touch of Honey

**Serves: 5**

**Cooking Time: 15 minutes**

**Ingredients:**

- 1/2 cup sorghum kernels
- 1/4 cup honey
- 2 tablespoons coconut oil
- Pinch of salt

**Instructions:**

- Pop sorghum kernels in a pot with coconut oil.
- Drizzle honey over the popped sorghum and mix well.
- Form the mixture into popcorn balls.

**Note (Ingredient Avoidance):**

*Kids should avoid regular popcorn because it can have gluten in the flavorings. Instead, we use sorghum to make our own popcorn balls - they're sweet, crunchy, and gluten-free!*

**Serving Suggestion:**

*Enjoy these honey-kissed popcorn balls during movie night for a gluten-free treat.*

**Nutritional Information:**

- Calories: 100 per serving
- Protein: 1g per serving
- Carbohydrates: 20g per serving
- Fat: 3g per serving
- Fiber: 2g per serving

# Teff and Vegetable Spring Rolls with Gluten-Free Dipping Sauce

**Serves: 6**

**Cooking Time: 30 minutes**

**Ingredients:**

- 12 rice paper wrappers
- 1 cup teff grains, cooked
- 1 cup julienned veggies (carrots, cucumbers, bell peppers)
- 1 cup lettuce, shredded
- Gluten-free soy sauce
- Sweet chili sauce
- Fresh mint leaves

**Instructions:**

- Dip a rice paper wrapper in warm water until it's soft.
- Lay it flat and add teff, veggies, and lettuce in the center.
- Fold the sides over the filling and roll it up like a burrito.

- Mix gluten-free soy sauce with sweet chili sauce for a tasty dipping sauce.

## Note (Ingredient Avoidance):

*Kids should avoid wheat and gluten because they can be tricky for tummies. Instead of regular spring roll wrappers, we use rice paper, which is super safe and fun to roll!*

## Serving Suggestion:

*Serve these spring rolls with the gluten-free dipping sauce and fresh mint leaves for a burst of flavor.*

## Nutritional Information:

- Calories: 150 per serving
- Protein: 4g per serving
- Carbohydrates: 32g per serving
- Fat: 1g per serving
- Fiber: 3g per serving

# Coconut Flour-Crusted Chicken Tenders with Honey Mustard Dip

**Serves: 4**

**Cooking Time: 25 minutes**

**Ingredients:**

- 1 pound chicken tenders
- 1 cup coconut flour
- 2 eggs
- Salt and pepper
- Cooking spray

*For Honey Mustard Dip:*

- 1/4 cup honey
- 2 tablespoons gluten-free mustard

**Instructions:**

- Preheat the oven to 400° F (200° C).
- Season chicken tenders with salt and pepper.
- Dip each tender in beaten eggs, then coat with coconut flour.

- Place on a baking sheet sprayed with cooking spray.
- Bake for 20 minutes or until golden brown.

## Note (Ingredient Avoidance):

*Kids should avoid wheat and gluten because they can be tricky for tummies. Instead of regular flour, we use coconut flour, making these chicken tenders extra crispy and safe!*

## Serving Suggestion:

*Serve these delicious chicken tenders with a side of honey mustard dip and some carrot sticks for a crunchy snack.*

## Nutritional Information:

- Calories: 250 per serving
- Protein: 20g per serving
- Carbohydrates: 16g per serving
- Fat: 12g per serving
- Fiber: 6g per serving

# Polenta and Pesto-Stuffed Cherry Tomatoes

**Serves: 4**

**Cooking Time: 15 minutes**

**Ingredients**:

- 20 cherry tomatoes
- 1 cup cooked polenta, cooled and sliced
- 1/2 cup gluten-free pesto
- Fresh basil leaves for garnish

**Instructions:**

- Cut a small slice off the bottom of each cherry tomato to make them stand upright.
- Scoop out the seeds and a bit of flesh from each tomato.
- Fill each tomato with a slice of polenta and top with a dollop of gluten-free pesto.
- Garnish with fresh basil leaves.

**Note (Ingredient Avoidance):**

*Kids should avoid wheat and gluten because they can be tricky for tummies. Instead of regular pesto, we use gluten-free pesto, and the polenta is a super fun and safe alternative!*

**Serving Suggestion:**

*Arrange these stuffed tomatoes on a colorful plate for a tasty and bite-sized treat.*

**Nutritional Information:**

- Calories: 120 per serving
- Protein: 3g per serving
- Carbohydrates: 18g per serving
- Fat: 5g per serving
- Fiber: 2g per serving

# Almond-Crusted Mozzarella Sticks with Marinara Sauce

**Serves: 4**

**Cooking Time: 20 minutes**

**Ingredients:**

- 8 mozzarella sticks
- 1 cup almond flour
- 2 eggs
- Salt and pepper
- Cooking spray

*For Marinara Sauce:*

- 1 cup gluten-free marinara sauce

**Instructions:**

- Preheat the oven to 375° F (190° C).
- Cut each mozzarella stick in half.
- Dip each stick in beaten eggs, then coat with almond flour.
- Place on a baking sheet sprayed with cooking spray.

- Bake for 15 minutes or until golden and gooey.

## Note (Ingredient Avoidance):

*Kids should avoid wheat and gluten because they can be tricky for tummies. Instead of regular flour, we use almond flour for an extra nutty crunch that's safe and tasty!*

## Serving Suggestion:

*Dip these almond-crusted mozzarella sticks in gluten-free marinara sauce for a yummy and cheesy snack.*

## Nutritional Information:

- Calories: 180 per serving
- Protein: 10g per serving
- Carbohydrates: 5g per serving
- Fat: 14g per serving
- Fiber: 2g per serving

# Chickpea Flour Savory Muffins with Spinach and Feta

**Serves: 6**

**Cooking Time: 30 minutes**

**Ingredients:**

- 1 cup chickpea flour
- 1/2 teaspoon baking powder
- 1/2 teaspoon baking soda
- 2 eggs
- 1/2 cup milk (or a non-dairy alternative)
- 1 cup fresh spinach, chopped
- 1/2 cup feta cheese, crumbled
- Salt and pepper to taste

**Instructions:**

- Preheat the oven to 375° F (190° C).
- In a bowl, whisk together chickpea flour, baking powder, and baking soda.
- In another bowl, beat the eggs and add milk.
- Mix the wet ingredients into the dry ingredients.

- Fold in chopped spinach and crumbled feta. Add salt and pepper to taste.
- Pour the batter into a greased muffin tin and bake for 20 minutes or until a toothpick comes out clean.

## Note (Ingredient Avoidance):

*Kids should avoid wheat and gluten because they can be tricky for tummies. Instead of regular flour, we use chickpea flour for these savory muffins. It's a magical substitute that's safe and delicious!*

## Serving Suggestion:

*Enjoy these muffins warm with a dollop of gluten-free hummus or a side of sliced veggies.*

## Nutritional Information:

- Calories: 120 per serving
- Protein: 7g per serving
- Carbohydrates: 12g per serving
- Fat: 5g per serving
- Fiber: 2g per serving

# CHAPTER 5

# DINNER RECIPES

*Quinoa-Stuffed Bell Peppers with Ground Turkey and Black Beans*

**Serves: 4**

**Cooking Time: 45 minutes**

**Ingredients:**

- 4 bell peppers (any color), halved and seeded
- 1 cup quinoa, rinsed
- 1 pound ground turkey
- 1 cup black beans, cooked
- 1 onion, diced
- 2 cloves garlic, minced
- 1 cup mixed veggies (carrots, peas, corn)
- 1 cup tomato sauce
- Salt and pepper to taste
- Olive oil

## Instructions:

- Preheat the oven to 375° F (190° C).
- Boil quinoa according to package instructions. Set aside.
- In a pan, cook ground turkey until browned. Set aside.
- In the same pan, sauté onions and garlic until soft. Add mixed veggies and cook until tender.
- Combine cooked quinoa, turkey, black beans, veggies, tomato sauce, salt, and pepper in a bowl.
- Rub bell pepper halves with olive oil and stuff them with the quinoa mixture.
- Place stuffed peppers in a baking dish, cover with foil, and bake for 25-30 minutes.

## Note (Ingredient Avoidance):

*Kids should avoid wheat, barley, and rye because they have gluten that can make tummies unhappy. Instead of breadcrumbs, we're using quinoa, which is safe and super yummy! Also, we've added black beans for extra fun and protein.*

**Serving Suggestion:**

*Serve these tasty stuffed peppers with a dollop of sour cream or a sprinkle of cheese for an extra treat.*

**Nutritional Information:**

- Calories: 360 per serving
- Protein: 22g per serving
- Carbohydrates: 45g per serving
- Fat: 11g per serving
- Fiber: 8g per serving

# Rice Noodle and Vegetable Stir-Fry with Gluten-Free Soy Sauce

**Serves: 4**

**Cooking Time: 30 minutes**

**Ingredients:**

- 8 oz rice noodles
- 2 cups mixed vegetables (broccoli, bell peppers, carrots)
- 1 cup snap peas, trimmed
- 1 cup gluten-free soy sauce
- 2 tablespoons vegetable oil
- 2 cloves garlic, minced
- 1 teaspoon ginger, grated
- Sesame seeds for garnish (optional)

**Instructions:**

- Cook rice noodles according to package instructions. Drain and set aside.
- In a large pan, heat vegetable oil over medium heat. Add garlic and ginger, sauté for 1-2 minutes.

- Add mixed vegetables and snap peas to the pan, stir-fry until tender-crisp.
- Pour gluten-free soy sauce over the veggies and stir to coat.
- Add the cooked rice noodles to the pan, toss everything together until well combined.
- Garnish with sesame seeds if you like.

## Note (Ingredient Avoidance):

*Kids, let's skip regular soy sauce because it has gluten. We're using a special gluten-free soy sauce that tastes just as awesome!*

## Serving Suggestion:

*Enjoy this colorful stir-fry on its own or with your favorite grilled protein, like chicken or shrimp.*

## Nutritional Information:

- Calories: 280 per serving
- Protein: 5g per serving
- Carbohydrates: 55g per serving
- Fat: 4g per serving

- Fiber: 3g per serving

## Lentil and Sweet Potato Curry with Basmati Rice

**Serves: 4**

**Cooking Time: 40 minutes**

**Ingredients:**

- 1 cup dry lentils, rinsed
- 2 medium-sized sweet potatoes, diced
- 1 onion, finely chopped
- 2 cloves garlic, minced
- 1 can (14 oz) coconut milk
- 1 cup vegetable broth
- 2 tablespoons curry powder
- 1 teaspoon turmeric
- Salt and pepper to taste
- 2 cups cooked basmati rice
- Fresh cilantro for garnish (optional)

## Instructions:

- In a pot, combine lentils, sweet potatoes, onion, garlic, coconut milk, vegetable broth, curry powder, turmeric, salt, and pepper.
- Bring to a boil, then reduce heat and simmer for 30 minutes or until lentils and sweet potatoes are tender.
- Serve the curry over a bed of cooked basmati rice.
- Garnish with fresh cilantro if you like.

## Note (Ingredient Avoidance):

*Kids, some lentils might have sneaky gluten friends, so always check the label. Also, watch out for curry powders that have added gluten. Our curry is safe, and it's like a flavor party in your mouth!*

## Serving Suggestion:

*This curry is extra tasty with a side of naan bread (make sure it's gluten-free) or a simple cucumber salad.*

## Nutritional Information:

- Calories: 420 per serving
- Protein: 12g per serving

- Carbohydrates: 75g per serving

- Fat: 8g per serving

- Fiber: 14g per serving

## *Zucchini Noodles with Gluten-Free Tomato Sauce and Grilled Shrimp*

**Serves: 4**

**Cooking Time: 25 minutes**

**Ingredients:**

- 4 medium-sized zucchinis, spiralized into noodles

- 1 pound shrimp, peeled and deveined

- 2 cups gluten-free tomato sauce

- 2 cloves garlic, minced

- 1 teaspoon dried oregano

- Salt and pepper to taste

- 2 tablespoons olive oil

- Fresh basil for garnish (optional)

- Grated Parmesan cheese (optional)

## Instructions:

- Heat olive oil in a pan over medium heat. Add minced garlic and sauté until fragrant.
- Add shrimp to the pan, sprinkle with salt, pepper, and dried oregano. Cook until shrimp turns pink and opaque.
- Pour gluten-free tomato sauce over the shrimp and let it simmer for 5 minutes.
- In a separate pan, sauté zucchini noodles for 2-3 minutes until they are just tender.
- Serve grilled shrimp on a bed of zucchini noodles and top with tomato sauce.
- Garnish with fresh basil and grated Parmesan if you like.

## Note (Ingredient Avoidance):

*Kids, regular pasta might make your tummy feel funny, but zucchini noodles are here to save the day! And the tomato sauce? No worries, it's gluten-free and delicious!*

**Serving Suggestion:**

*Pair this dish with a side of your favorite gluten-free garlic bread or a simple green salad.*

**Nutritional Information:**

- Calories: 320 per serving
- Protein: 25g per serving
- Carbohydrates: 20g per serving
- Fat: 15g per serving
- Fiber: 5g per serving

# Buckwheat and Vegetable Risotto with Parmesan Cheese

**Serves: 4**

**Cooking Time: 35 minutes**

**Ingredients:**

- 1 cup buckwheat groats
- 4 cups vegetable broth
- 1 onion, finely chopped
- 2 cloves garlic, minced
- 1 cup mixed vegetables (peas, carrots, corn)
- 1/2 cup Parmesan cheese, grated
- 2 tablespoons olive oil
- Salt and pepper to taste
- Fresh parsley for garnish (optional)

**Instructions:**

- In a pot, heat olive oil over medium heat. Add chopped onions and garlic, sauté until they become soft and translucent.

- Add buckwheat groats to the pot and toast for 2-3 minutes.
- Gradually add vegetable broth, one cup at a time, stirring frequently. Allow the liquid to absorb before adding the next cup.
- When the buckwheat is almost tender, add mixed vegetables and continue cooking until the buckwheat is fully cooked and has a creamy consistency.
- Stir in grated Parmesan cheese and season with salt and pepper to taste.
- Garnish with fresh parsley if you like.

## Note (Ingredient Avoidance):

*Kids, some grains have tricky gluten, but not our friend buckwheat! It's safe and super tasty. And the Parmesan cheese? No gluten worries there!*

## Serving Suggestion:

*This risotto is perfect on its own or paired with a side of steamed broccoli or a fresh garden salad.*

## Nutritional Information:

- Calories: 290 per serving
- Protein: 10g per serving
- Carbohydrates: 40g per serving
- Fat: 10g per serving
- Fiber: 7g per serving

## Millet-Crusted Chicken Breasts with Roasted Vegetables

**Serves: 4**

**Cooking Time: 40 minutes**

**Ingredients:**

- 4 boneless, skinless chicken breasts
- 1 cup millet, ground into flour
- 2 eggs
- Salt and pepper to taste
- Assorted vegetables (carrots, bell peppers, zucchini)
- Olive oil

## Instructions:

- Preheat the oven to 400° F (200° C).
- Season chicken breasts with salt and pepper.
- Dip each chicken breast in beaten eggs, then coat with millet flour.
- Place the coated chicken on a baking sheet and surround with chopped vegetables.
- Drizzle olive oil over the chicken and veggies.
- Roast in the oven for 25-30 minutes or until the chicken is cooked through.

## Note (Ingredient Avoidance):

*Kids should avoid wheat, barley, and rye because they can be tricky for tummies. Instead of regular flour, we use ground millet, which is not only safe but gives the chicken a yummy crunchy coating!*

## Serving Suggestion:

*Serve these crispy chicken breasts with a side of colorful roasted veggies for a delicious and healthy meal.*

## Nutritional Information:

- Calories: 350 per serving
- Protein: 30g per serving
- Carbohydrates: 25g per serving
- Fat: 15g per serving
- Fiber: 5g per serving

## *Sorghum Grain Bowl with Grilled Chicken and Avocado*

**Serves: 4**

**Cooking Time: 35 minutes**

**Ingredients:**

- 1 cup sorghum grains, cooked
- 1 pound chicken breasts, grilled and sliced
- 1 avocado, sliced
- Cherry tomatoes, halved
- Cucumber, diced
- Olive oil
- Lemon juice
- Salt and pepper to taste

## Instructions:

- Cook sorghum grains according to package instructions.
- Grill chicken breasts until fully cooked, then slice them into strips.
- In a bowl, mix cooked sorghum, grilled chicken, avocado slices, cherry tomatoes, and cucumber.
- Drizzle with olive oil and lemon juice, then season with salt and pepper.

## Note (Ingredient Avoidance):

*Kids should skip wheat, barley, and rye because they can be like little troublemakers for sensitive tummies. Instead of those, we're using sorghum, which is not only safe but super tasty!*

## Serving Suggestion:

*Enjoy this colorful bowl with a squeeze of lemon juice for a zesty kick.*

## Nutritional Information:

- Calories: 320 per serving

- Protein: 25g per serving

- Carbohydrates: 40g per serving

- Fat: 10g per serving

- Fiber: 8g per serving

## *Teff and Salmon Patties with Dill Sauce*

**Serves: 4**

**Cooking Time: 30 minutes**

**Ingredients:**

- 1 cup teff flour

- 2 cans (14 oz each) canned salmon, drained

- 1/2 cup chopped green onions

- 2 eggs

- 2 tablespoons chopped fresh dill

- Salt and pepper to taste

- Olive oil

**Instructions:**

- In a bowl, mix teff flour, canned salmon, green onions, eggs, dill, salt, and pepper.

- Form the mixture into patties.

- Heat olive oil in a pan over medium heat.
- Cook the patties for 3-4 minutes on each side or until golden brown.

## Note (Ingredient Avoidance):

*Kids should steer clear of wheat, barley, and rye because they can be tricky for tiny tummies. Instead, we're using teff flour, which is not only safe but adds a nutty flavor to our yummy salmon patties!*

## Serving Suggestion:

*Serve these delicious salmon patties with a dollop of dill sauce for extra flavor.*

## Nutritional Information:

- Calories: 280 per serving
- Protein: 20g per serving
- Carbohydrates: 25g per serving
- Fat: 12g per serving
- Fiber: 6g per serving

# Coconut Flour-Crusted Tilapia with Quinoa Pilaf

**Serves: 4**

**Cooking Time: 25 minutes**

**Ingredients:**

- 4 tilapia fillets
- 1/2 cup coconut flour
- 2 eggs
- 1 cup quinoa, cooked
- Mixed vegetables (peas, carrots, corn)
- Coconut oil
- Lemon wedges
- Salt and pepper to taste

**Instructions:**

- Preheat the oven to 375° F (190° C).
- In one bowl, place coconut flour. In another, beat the eggs.
- Dip each tilapia fillet in the egg, then coat with coconut flour.

- Heat coconut oil in a pan over medium heat.
- Cook tilapia for 2-3 minutes on each side until golden.
- In a separate pan, sauté mixed vegetables and mix them with cooked quinoa.

**Note (Ingredient Avoidance):**

*Kids should skip wheat, barley, and rye because they can be like little rascals for delicate tummies. Instead of regular flour, we're using coconut flour, which gives our tilapia a special, yummy crunch!*

**Serving Suggestion:**

*Serve these crispy tilapia fillets on a bed of quinoa pilaf with a squeeze of lemon for a tropical twist.*

**Nutritional Information**:

- Calories: 320 per serving
- Protein: 25g per serving
- Carbohydrates: 30g per serving
- Fat: 15g per serving
- Fiber: 5g per serving

## Polenta Lasagna with Layers of Marinara, Spinach, and Cheese

**Serves: 6**

**Cooking Time: 50 minutes**

**Ingredients:**

- 2 cups polenta, cooked and sliced
- 2 cups gluten-free marinara sauce
- 2 cups fresh spinach leaves
- 2 cups shredded mozzarella cheese
- 1 cup grated Parmesan cheese
- Olive oil
- Italian seasoning
- Salt and pepper to taste

**Instructions:**

- Preheat the oven to 375° F (190° C).
- In a baking dish, layer sliced polenta, marinara sauce, spinach, and cheeses.
- Repeat the layers, finishing with a generous sprinkle of mozzarella and Parmesan on top.

- Drizzle with olive oil and sprinkle Italian seasoning, salt, and pepper.
- Bake in the oven for 30-35 minutes or until the cheese is bubbly and golden.

**Note (Ingredient Avoidance):**

*Kids should stay away from wheat, barley, and rye because they can be a bit tricky for little tummies. Instead of regular lasagna noodles, we're using polenta, which is not only safe but gives our lasagna a fantastic texture!*

**Serving Suggestion:**

*Serve this cheesy polenta lasagna with a side salad for a delightful and comforting meal.*

**Nutritional Information:**

- Calories: 380 per serving
- Protein: 20g per serving
- Carbohydrates: 35g per serving
- Fat: 18g per serving
- Fiber: 5g per serving

# BONUS 1

# 7 DAYS MEAL PLAN

*Day 1*

**Breakfast**: Gluten-free Pancakes with Almond Flour

**Lunch**: Quinoa-Stuffed Bell Peppers with Ground Turkey and Veggies

**Snack**: Rice Cake with Almond Butter and Sliced Strawberries

**Dinner**: Quinoa-Stuffed Bell Peppers with Ground Turkey and Black Beans

*Day 2*

**Breakfast**: Quinoa Breakfast Bowl with Fruits and Nuts

**Lunch**: Rice Noodle Stir-Fry with Gluten-Free Soy Sauce and Vegetables

**Snack**: Quinoa and Black Bean Salsa with Gluten-Free Tortilla Chips

**Dinner**: Rice Noodle and Vegetable Stir-Fry with Gluten-Free Soy Sauce

## Day 3

**Breakfast**: Rice Flour Crepes with Strawberry Filling

**Lunch**: Lentil and Vegetable Curry with Basmati Rice

**Snack**: Buckwheat Crackers with Hummus

**Dinner**: Lentil and Sweet Potato Curry with Basmati Rice

## Day 4

**Breakfast**: Buckwheat Waffles Topped with Blueberries

**Lunch**: Zucchini Noodles with Gluten-Free Tomato Sauce and Grilled Chicken

**Snack**: Millet Energy Bites with Dried Fruit and Seeds

**Dinner**: Zucchini Noodles with Gluten-Free Tomato Sauce and Grilled Shrimp

## Day 5

**Breakfast**: Millet Porridge with Cinnamon and Apples

**Lunch**: Buckwheat and Vegetable Sushi Rolls

**Snack**: Sorghum Popcorn Balls with a Touch of Honey

**Dinner**: Buckwheat and Vegetable Risotto with Parmesan Cheese

## Day 6

**Breakfast**: Sorghum Cereal with Banana Slices

**Lunch**: Millet and Black Bean Salad with Lime Vinaigrette

**Snack**: Teff and Vegetable Spring Rolls with Gluten-Free Dipping Sauce

**Dinner**: Millet-Crusted Chicken Breasts

## Day 7

**Breakfast**: Teff Muffins with Raspberries

**Lunch**: Sorghum Grain Bowl with Roasted Vegetables and Tahini Dressing

**Snack**: Coconut Flour-Crusted Chicken Tenders with Honey Mustard Dip

**Dinner**: Coconut Flour-Crusted Tilapia with Quinoa Pilaf

# BONUS 2

## AMELIA SOPHIA
# WEEKLY FOOD JOURNAL

WEEK: ONE

| | |
|---|---|
| Breakfast<br>Lunch<br>Dinner<br>Snacks<br>Rate your day ○○○○○ | Breakfast<br>Lunch<br>Dinner<br>Snacks<br>Rate your day ○○○○○ |
| Breakfast<br>Lunch<br>Dinner<br>Snacks<br>Rate your day ○○○○○ | Breakfast<br>Lunch<br>Dinner<br>Snacks<br>Rate your day ○○○○○ |
| Breakfast<br>Lunch<br>Dinner<br>Snacks<br>Rate your day ○○○○○ | Breakfast<br>Lunch<br>Dinner<br>Snacks<br>Rate your day ○○○○○ |
| Breakfast<br>Lunch<br>Dinner<br>Snacks<br>Rate your day ○○○○○ | NOTES: |

# AMELIA SOPHIA
# WEEKLY FOOD JOURNAL

WEEK: TWO

Breakfast
Lunch
Dinner
Snacks

Rate your day ○○○○○

Breakfast
Lunch
Dinner
Snacks

Rate your day ○○○○○

Breakfast
Lunch
Dinner
Snacks
Rate your day ○○○○○

Breakfast
Lunch
Dinner
Snacks

Rate your day ○○○○○

Breakfast
Lunch
Dinner
Snacks

Rate your day ○○○○○

Breakfast
Lunch
Dinner
Snacks

Rate your day ○○○○○

Breakfast
Lunch
Dinner
Snacks

Rate your day ○○○○○

NOTES:

# AMELIA SOPHIA

# WEEKLY FOOD JOURNAL

### WEEK: THREE

Breakfast
Lunch
Dinner
Snacks

Rate your day ○○○○○

Breakfast
Lunch
Dinner
Snacks

Rate your day ○○○○○

Breakfast
Lunch
Dinner
Snacks

Rate your day ○○○○○

Breakfast
Lunch
Dinner
Snacks

Rate your day ○○○○○

Breakfast
Lunch
Dinner
Snacks

Rate your day ○○○○○

Breakfast
Lunch
Dinner
Snacks

Rate your day ○○○○○

Breakfast
Lunch
Dinner
Snacks

Rate your day ○○○○○

NOTES:

# AMELIA SOPHIA
# WEEKLY FOOD JOURNAL

### WEEK: FOUR

| | |
|---|---|
| Breakfast | Breakfast |
| Lunch | Lunch |
| Dinner | Dinner |
| Snacks | Snacks |
| Rate your day ○○○○○ | Rate your day ○○○○○ |

| | |
|---|---|
| Breakfast | Breakfast |
| Lunch | Lunch |
| Dinner | Dinner |
| Snacks | Snacks |
| Rate your day ○○○○○ | Rate your day ○○○○○ |

| | |
|---|---|
| Breakfast | Breakfast |
| Lunch | Lunch |
| Dinner | Dinner |
| Snacks | Snacks |
| Rate your day ○○○○○ | Rate your day ○○○○○ |

Breakfast

Lunch

Dinner

Snacks

Rate your day ○○○○○

NOTES:

## *ASKING FOR AN HONEST REVIEW*

I wanted to reach out and personally thank you for taking the time to explore the world of flavors and creations that I poured into those pages.

Your experience matters a lot to me, and I would be truly grateful if you could share your honest thoughts in a review. Whether it's a brief note or a detailed reflection, your feedback will not only help me grow as a creator but also guide fellow food enthusiasts in deciding if this cookbook is a culinary adventure they'd like to embark on.

Feel free to highlight your favorite recipes, share any challenges you conquered, or even suggest what you'd love to see more of in future editions. Your unique perspective adds a special spice to the whole mix!

Thank you again for being a part of this delicious journey. I can't wait to hear what you think!

## About the author

As an author, Amelia weaves together her expertise in nutrition with her creative flair, penning cookbooks that not only tantalize taste buds but also empower readers to make mindful choices about what they put on their plates. Her writing style is a delightful blend of culinary expertise and a sprinkle of literary magic.

Amelia Sophia's cookbooks are more than just collections of recipes—they're invitations to embark on a flavorful journey, exploring the intersection of health and gastronomy. Her words inspire readers to savor each bite, knowing that nourishing the body can be a delicious and fulfilling adventure.

Whether she's crafting a tantalizing recipe or composing a prose that celebrates the beauty of mindful eating, Amelia Sophia's work reflects her commitment to a wholesome, balanced life. So, embark on a literary and culinary adventure with Amelia Sophia, and discover the joy of feeding.

Printed in Great Britain
by Amazon

44217700R00066